Tennessee Travel Guide

A Traveler's Tour Guide

With

History and Insider Tips

For Perfect Vacation.

Willard Turner

A SPECIAL REQUEST

Greetings and thank you for acquiring this book! Your prompt review on Amazon can provide valuable insights. The process is straightforward: navigate to the ORDER section in your Amazon account and select the "write a review for the product" option. This will promptly direct you to the review section. We look forward to hearing from you!

Table of Contents

Welcome To Tennessee

Chapter 1

    History
    Climate and weather
    Facts You Should Know About Tennessee

Chapter 2

    Getting to Tennessee
    Visa Requirements
    The Ideal Season To Visit Tennessee
    Packing For Tennesse
    Traveling Cost To Tennessee
    When Is the Best Time to Travel to Tennessee?
    Budget For Traveling Throughout Tennessee

Chapter 3

    How to Navigate Tennessee
    Accommodations In Tennessee
    Recommended Things To Do In Tennessee
    Top Rated Tourist Attractions in Tennessee

Tennessee's Bars and Pubs With Best Spots
Tennessee Dining and Cuisine With Best Spots
What You Shouldn't Miss When Visiting Tennessee

Chapter 4

Check-out My Choicest Restaurants
Shopping And Leisure With Best Spots
Best Beaches in Tennessee To Visit
Pay A Visit To The Museums

Chapter 5

Top Insider's Tips and Tricks For Tennessee
Currency And Money
Language
Slang words to use when you travel to Tennessee:
Vaccinations
Online accessibility
Transportation
Holidays And Festivals
Contact Numbers
Budget Tips

Welcome To Tennessee

The sun was sinking low on the horizon, casting a warm, golden glow across the Tennessee hills. As cars crossed the state line, anticipation was in the air. From Tennessee, a state renowned for its extensive history and warm southern hospitality, greetings.

Nestled in the center of the American South, Tennessee drew visitors in with its diverse landscape, which included the Mississippi River and the Great Smoky Mountains. Visitors came from all over the country and the globe to enjoy the state's distinct charms.

Many began their journey in Memphis, which is well-known for its soulful music and succulent BBQ. The night was brightened by neon lights, street corners featured live music, and Beale Street—the original home of the blues—was bustling with bustle. The globe flocked to Graceland, the former home of Rock 'n' Roll King Elvis Presley, to witness his live performances.

The scenery changed as you traveled east, with the Great Smoky Mountains rising like ancient sentinels on the horizon. Hiking trails meandered through the lush forests, offering views of cascading waterfalls and vast vistas. The area's bubbling brooks and rustling leaves were living examples of the beauty of nature.

Nashville, the capital city of the country, was the center of the country music scene. Grand Ole Opry, the legendary radio show, has created countless careers and is a revered forum for musicians even now. Honky-tonks dotted Broadway, where aspiring musicians gave their best performances in the hopes of getting their big break.

Knoxville, which was nestled beneath the Smoky Mountains, offered a special fusion of the modern and the historic. The University of Tennessee campus was alive with the excitement of students, and local artists' talents were on exhibit at the outdoor markets in Market Square.

Chattanooga was a city that had embraced its industrial past and developed into a hub for innovation and outdoor activities, with its renovated riverfront and well-known incline train.

In Tennessee, hello and "howdy" were the standard greetings; traditions were strongly rooted and sweet tea was abundant. There, the echoes of the past and the dreams for the future merged to create a setting full of vivid storytelling.

Tennessee boasts heartfelt music, cozy cuisine, and a distinctly Southern vibe that is evident throughout the entire region. In the next chapters, we'll go deeper into Tennessee's rich history, gorgeous landscape, and diverse culture. Together, these factors make Tennessee a very remarkable place to visit.

Chapter 1

History

Tennessee was initially and primarily inhabited by several Indian tribes. The Chickamaugas lived near Chattanooga, the Creeks lived farther down the Tennessee River, partially in Alabama, and the Cherokees, the most warlike, lived in the mountains to the east, with Kentucky on one side and Georgia on the other. The Chickasaws lived in and around Memphis. The Uchen was from the Nashville region. These people lived in a vast wilderness rich with wildlife and luscious forests.

When European hunters from Virginia and North Carolina discovered this vast wilderness abounding with deer and buffalo, they ventured into the treacherous and disputed territory.

William Bean of Virginia established the first colony on the Watauga River when he constructed his log cabin at the mouth of Hoone's Creek. His family moved in in 1769. Russel Bean, his son, was born here, becoming Tennessee's first known white child.

This was the beginning of Tennessee's history. On their voyages, the Indians used "The Great Trace" route. This route ran across East Tennessee and connected the Southwest to the North. The claim to what is now Tennessee was contested for a long time. The United Kingdom's King Charles II claimed all land on the North American Continent founded by his subjects. He gave out vast tracts of land, sometimes to individuals, sometimes to corporations and enterprises. He argued that only he could gain land from the Indians.

North Carolina, which included Tennessee, was given to a group of renowned Englishmen. The English established a policy of fortification. In 1756, Fort Loudon became the first fort in East Tennessee.

Hostilities between white men and Indians began when, on their journey back from Virginia, the Cherokees saw six horses grazing free and, mistaking them for wild, captured them. The Indians were murdered because the owners mistook them for horse thieves. In retribution, the Indians massacred whatever Europeans they could find. They stormed Fort Loudon and murdered everyone save for one officer and twenty men who lived to tell the tale.

By 1768, many pioneers had moved from older villages to the Tennessee Valley, where they could find cheap land. The most expensive price they paid was the genuine pain and risk they had to undergo to rescue their houses.

Pioneers from Virginia and North Carolina started building cabins along the Holston and Watauga rivers, and by 1770, there was a sizable population.

Despite being a part of North Carolina, the settlers south of the Holston and along the Wataugs had essentially no form of government. In response to the Anglo-Saxon race's strong desire for self-government, these brave pioneers gathered in 1772 on the Watauga, where Elizabethton currently lies, and formed the "Watauga Association." This was Tennessee's initial seat of government, and it lasted until August 1776, when the region known as the "Washington District" was annexed to North Carolina and transformed into a county of the same name, comprising the whole modern state of Tennessee.

Two years later, in 1778, Tennessee's first town, Jonesborough (now Jonesboro), was established as the county's first seat of government.

The Washington District was given to the United States in June 1784 by an act of the North Carolina Legislature, subject to acceptance within two years. The Wataugans were upset that they had been thrown off without consultation and were anxious about their current predicament. Representatives from three of the four counties in the "Washington District" convened in Jonesboro on August 23, 1784.

These forty representatives elected John Sevier as president and formed an organization to plan the formation of a new state as well as to prepare for a subsequent convention to adopt a constitution and establish a new government. Franklin was named after Benjamin Franklin, and Governor John Sevier was elected.

This was Tennessee's first legislative Assembly, and Greenville was designated as the state capital. In November 1784, the North Carolina General Assembly repealed the act of cession and reclaimed authority of the Western Territory, culminating in a political power struggle. People began to reject the Franklin Administration in favor of the state of North Carolina. In March 1778, Sevier's mandate expired, and the State of Franklin perished. In 1789, John Sevier was elected to Congress to represent the Mississippi Valley. Two years later, in 1790, it became the Territory of the United States South of the Ohio River and remained thus until June 1, 1796, when Tennessee was admitted as the sixteenth state to the Union.

Climate and weather

Tennessee's climate is humid subtropical, with hot and humid summers and relatively mild winters. Summer temperatures can reach the 90s Fahrenheit, while winter temperatures seldom fall below freezing. Rainfall is plentiful throughout the year, giving Tennessee an ideal site for producing crops and flowers. In addition, the state offers four distinct seasons, with vibrant foliage in the fall and snow-capped mountains in the winter. Tornadoes can also occur in select areas of Tennessee during the spring months. Tennessee's climate is temperate and pleasant enough to entice visitors all year.

Tennessee receives precipitation on an average of 116 days per year. Precipitation is defined as rain, snow, sleet, or hail that falls to the earth. You must have at least.01 inches of precipitation on the ground to count it.

Summer maximum: The maximum temperature in July is around 88 degrees.
The low temperature in January is 27 degrees Fahrenheit.
Rainfall: 53 inches per year on average
Snowfall: 5 inches per year on average

Facts You Should Know About Tennessee

1.   It is the birthplace of Mountain Dew.

This Appalachian delicacy's original recipe was created in the 1940s. Beverage bottlers Barney and Ally Hartman initially advertised their sweet drink in three locations, two of which were Knoxville and Johnson City. The drink's success did not endure long, as it was eventually purchased by Pepsi-Cola in 1964, introducing Mountain Dew to the rest of the world.

2.   It also has the distinction of having the most boundaries.

Tennessee is bounded to the north by Kentucky and Virginia, to the east by North Carolina, to the west by Arkansas and Missouri, and the south by Georgia, Mississippi, and Alabama. Missouri is the only other state with such a diverse range of interests.

3.   True Tennessee whiskey can only be produced in the state of Tennessee.

Tennessee whiskey is more than just a name. It's a separate whiskey made using the famed "Lincoln County Process," which includes a charcoal filter and strict age and timing parameters. Although several brands have the official "Tennessee whiskey" logo, the famed Jack Daniels brand accounts for the majority of the state's whiskey exports.

4. It is home to the world's oldest radio show.

The Grand Ole Opry is a country music show. The Opry is a landmark in the music industry as well as a destination for country music fans. The Grand Ole Opry, presently situated in Nashville, is the world's longest-running radio show. Every year, 6,000 songs are performed at the venue, which is a major tourist attraction in the city.

5. Cotton candy was invented at this location.

The exquisite dessert was conceived in Nashville by an unlikely duo: a dentist and a candy producer. The earliest markers were created by Dr. William Morrison and John Wharton, who melted sugar crystals and blew them over a screen to create tiny threads. It first appeared at the 1904 St. Louis Fair and rapidly sold out.

6.   The Moon Pie

This chocolate-covered snack cake was invented in a Chattanooga bakery in 1917 and quickly became a local favorite. It was a popular item among regular clients, and hundreds were being made in-house by the late 1920s. During World War II, the pie was also employed as a suitable ration item for troops and women serving overseas.

7. It has over 10,000 caves and caverns.

Tennessee is beautiful on the surface, but many people miss out on some of its hidden gems. The state contains 10,000 caves and caverns, many of which are thousands of years old and attract spelunkers from all across the country.

8. Bristol, not Nashville, is where country music began.

Bristol, on the Tennessee-Virginia border, is noted for its folk and blues music and is located in the heart of Appalachia. In the early days of the recording industry, Ralph Peer of Victor Records chose to record local artists in Bristol, and he secured two contracts that resulted in nationally successful albums. Those early contracts and recordings provided the framework for the country genre. To preserve this important piece of music history, Congress passed a resolution in 1998 naming Bristol the "Birthplace of Country Music." The city has its museum and a music festival that attracts country music fans year after year.

9. Bakersville is also the birthplace of Hattie Caraway, America's first female senator, who was born in 1878.

She went on to become the first woman in the country to be elected (and re-elected!) to a full term as an Arkansas

U.S. Senator. The state's distillery industry suffered greatly as a result of Prohibition.

Before the Civil War, whiskey and moonshine were common in Tennessee. In 1908, there were hundreds of registered distilleries in the state, but many of them were destroyed when the state imposed prohibition legislation as early as 1910. While some were reopened in the 1940s and 1990s, it wasn't until 2009 that enough legal reforms were put in place to abolish the majority of entrance barriers. As a result, there are currently over 30 distilleries to visit on the Tennessee Whiskey Trail.

Elvis Presley's old home is the country's second most visited house museum.

Elvis Presley's world-famous estate, Graceland, is a Memphis institution. You may be surprised to learn that it is also the country's second-most visited house museum. Every year, it draws roughly 600,000 visitors, second only to the White House.

10. Tin Pan South is the largest songwriter's festival in the world.

Tin Pan South is a music and songwriters event held in Nashville, Tennessee every year. The annual five-day festival, which features diverse types of music, takes place in a variety of sites across the city.

11. It is home to the most visited national park in the country.

This honor goes to the one and only Great Smoky Mountains National Park. This park is by far the most frequented in the country; in 2020, it will attract more than twice the number of visitors (12.1 million) as runner-up Yellowstone. It is also known as the "Salamander Capital of the World" since it is home to 30 different species of this amphibian.

12. The Tennessee River serves as a vital economic waterway.

The Tennessee Waterway, the longest tributary of the Ohio River, is still a significant commercial and industrial waterway. Every year, an estimated 28,000 barges navigate the river, hauling 45 to 50 million tons of cargo.

Chapter 2

Getting To Tennessee

By Car

Interstate 40 extends from west to east throughout the state, connecting Memphis, Nashville, Knoxville, and the Smoky Mountain Region. Interstate 55 entirely encircles Memphis. Interstate 155 stretches from Missouri to Dyersburg in northwest Tennessee. Interstate 24 starts in Kentucky near Clarksville and ends in Chattanooga (after briefly crossing into Georgia for roughly three miles / five kilometers). Interstate 65 runs through Nashville on its journey from Kentucky to Alabama. Interstate 75, which begins in Kentucky, links Knoxville with Chattanooga before crossing into Georgia. Interstate 81 begins on Interstate 40 in Knoxville and proceeds northeast to Bristol before entering Virginia. Interstate 26 runs south from Interstate 81 into North Carolina (towards Asheville) in the Kingsport region, whereas Interstate 181 continues north from Interstate 81 into Kingsport and the Virginia state line.

By Plane

The state has many airports. Memphis International Airport is served by several major airlines, however, it only has one international flight (as of November 2019) to Toronto, Canada. Nashville Foreign Airport acts as a hub for Southwest Airlines and is served by several other domestic and foreign airlines, with nonstop flights to Canada, Mexico, Jamaica, The Bahamas, the Dominican Republic, the United Kingdom, and Germany. Air service is provided by smaller airports at Maryville (Knoxville), Chattanooga, and Bristol. Southern Tennessee has easy access to the Huntsville, Alabama, airport.

Tennessee Amtrak service is limited to New Orleans, with stops at Memphis and Newbern.

By Bus

Greyhound bus service is available across Tennessee. Megabus operates routes to Memphis, Nashville (from Atlanta), Chattanooga (from Atlanta), and Knoxville (from Washington, D.C., Christiansburg, and Atlanta) from Chicago, Champaign-Urbana, St. Louis, Atlanta, Birmingham, Dallas, and Little Rock.

Visa Requirements

Tennessee has many reasons to live there, but it also has many reasons to visit. A temporary visa, sometimes known as a "visitor visa," allows persons from other countries to stay in the United States for lengthy periods without giving up their citizenship in their home country. The Law Office of Perry A. Craft, PLLC may assist you if you need a temporary visa for a business seminar, an extended vacation, or a celebratory event such as a wedding. We answer your questions about the visa application process, how long it takes, and how long you may remain in the country.

What documentation is needed for a temporary visa?

A non-immigrant visa is intended for people who wish to visit America but do not want to remain permanently. Because overseas travel rules might be complicated, be sure you have all of your documentation in order. Come to our office, and Attorney Perry A. Craft will guide you through the whole procedure. To apply, you must generally:

Complete the visa application.

Make the application fee payment. Keep the receipt in case you ever need to prove that you paid the amount.

Have a passport that is valid for another six months after you leave the country; for example, if you plan to stay in Tennessee for a year, you must have an 18-month passport.

Bring a photo ID.

Take part in an interview at a consulate. You will be fingerprinted during this interview, and you should be prepared to answer questions about where you are going, how long you intend to stay, and how you intend to pay for what you need while you are there.

What kind of B visa do you need?

B1 and B2 non-immigrant visas are available. A B1 temporary visa is only for business purposes, although the rules are fairly strict. A B1 visa is often the ideal option if you are attending a conference, consulting with your overseas business partners, or playing in an exhibition game. You may not be paid by an American corporation while on this temporary visa, but you may be paid by your own company in your home country.

Tourists and travelers must get a B2 visa. The B2 temporary visa is excellent for attending a wedding, taking a vacation, or competing in amateur sports events. A B2 visa can also be granted if you need a specialized medical operation or treatment, or if you want to attend a conference for entertainment purposes.

You may be eligible to apply for a B1/B2 visa if you plan to combine work and pleasure throughout your stay. Depending on how frequently you renew your B visa, it can be valid for up to 10 years. At the Law Office of Perry A. Craft, PLLC, we can assist you in deciding whether a temporary visa or a permanent visa is more suited to your needs.

The Ideal Season To Visit Tennessee

Although you may visit Tennessee at any time, the best time to visit Tennessee is determined by your trip goals. The months of March to May, as well as September to November, are considered the most pleasant, with temperate days, cool evenings, and a moderate level of humidity. Nothing beats looking at blooming flowers in the spring or fall leaves. The views from Clingman's Dome are stunning in all four seasons. June and August are often the busiest months. To cool down and relax in the heat, explore Fall Creek Falls and Machine Falls. The tourist rush has eased by the time winter arrives, and it's time to go the Little River Road to view the Smokies at their best.

Packing For Tennessee

Clothes

Clothes Depending on the season, you'll need to layer up or wear looser, lighter clothing. From April through October, average highs and lows are in the upper 40s to upper 60s. The lower 70s to the upper 80s are the typical daytime highs.

What clothes are typical in Nashville? In any case, describe the Nashville style in detail. It seems fitting that Nashville's design would have a greater hipster leaning with a splash of Western flare since the city is widely recognized for its live music culture. Wearing pants and a stylish top will help you seem regular when you go out. In Nashville, Tennessee, flowing denim works well with everything, but if the weather permits, you may also accessorize the basics with a stylish twist or wear sundresses with floral designs.

Do you have trouble dressing appropriately for October in Tennessee? For October travel, a denim jacket is a great complement to have on hand for Tennessee's brisk days and chilly nights. The same advice holds if you're wondering what to wear in September in Tennessee. If you want to stay in Tennessee for many weeks or more, make sure to include additional jackets in your list of things to pack.

However, between November and March, visitors should expect temperatures in the mid-20s to high 50s. As with any vacation, look out for the local weather forecast before you pack or decide what to wear to a Tennessee nighttime event.

Having the following clothing on hand will ensure that your trip is comfortable:

- Bottoms with Underslips
- (Sports, casual, denim, etc.) shorts
- tops of t-shirts with tanks
- Pullovers and Pullover shirts
- Sleeping clothes
- Wool socks for winter.

- Pullovers
- Sneakers or Boots for Hiking Shoes for Comfy Walking
- Winter Showers Beanie, Jacket, Gloves, Scarf, and Cap
- Intimate Sunglasses

Are you not sure what Tennessee requires you to wear? Excessive use of animal patterns or the wearing of black leather cowboy boots and headgear might be seductive. On the other hand, unless they are well-known country music performers, Tennesseeans often wear casual attire. It will look fantastic with slim jeans and a cozy graphic shirt!

Toiletries

Do you have any questions regarding what personal hygiene items to pack for Tennessee? Be advised that most hotels provide free bath items to their guests, among other amenities. As a consequence, you might not even need to pack shampoo, conditioner, and/or soap.

If you're worried, you may call the front desk in advance to find out what services your hotel offers.

Given that, you may choose to bring the following necessities for your trip:

- Using toothbrush and toothpaste
- spectacles
- Antiseptic Shampoo
- Hair conditioner, face wash soap, shaving cream, and razors
- Sunscreen
- Cosmetics
- A hairbrush and dryer
- Hair Care Products
- Personal Medicines

Outdoor Gear

Before you head out into the great outdoors, remember to check what you'll need for your vacation to Tennessee! Your choice of outdoor activities will determine what you should pack for your trip to

Tennessee. Regardless of the activity, there are always some essentials for outdoor clothing that you should never leave home without.

Beautiful parks in Tennessee provide a nice diversion from the metropolis. Night hiking is permitted even in locations like Warner Park Nature Center, Owl's Hill Nature Sanctuary, and Bells Bend Nature Park. Thus, if you do decide to go outside, make sure you have Tennessee essentials with you.

Here is a potential list of items to carry for an outdoor trip:
Sports Gear: Refillable Water Bottle, Bug Repellent, Hammock, and Daypack.

Miscellaneous

Depending on how you want to utilize your trip, there may be differences in what you need to bring.
Consider including the following items on your packing list for Tennessee:

- Additional batteries and camera charger books
- Laptop and Charger
- Additional Baggage to Return with Keepsakes

To have the best trip possible, make sure you bring everything on this list, and don't forget to include anything more you might need. Remember that your Tennessee vacation should be customized to meet your needs!

Traveling Cost To Tennessee

A seven-day trip to Tennessee costs $1,077 on average for a single traveler, $1,626 for a couple, and $3,204 for a family of four. Tennessee hotels cost between $57 and $260 a night, with an average of $88, but most vacation homes cost between $180 and $620 per night for the entire property. The average global travel cost to Tennessee (from all airports) ranges from $556 to $878 per person in economy and $1,746 to $2,757 in first class. Depending on your interests, we recommend spending $44 to $89 per person per day for transportation and meals at local restaurants.

When Is the Best Time to Travel to Tennessee?

On average, the following are the cheapest dates to fly to Tennessee and stay at a Tennessee hotel:

January 8th through March 11th, April 16th through April 29th, and August 6th through December 9th (except November 26th)

Early to mid-September is frequently the most cost-effective time to visit Tennessee.

Budget For Traveling Throughout Tennessee

For your Tennessee vacation, you should budget $172 every day. This is the average daily price based on the prices of other visitors. Previous visitors have spent, on average, the following on a single day:

$41 was spent on food.

Local transportation costs $21.

$198 in hotel expenses.

On average, a one-week trip to Tennessee for two people costs around $2,409. This includes accommodations, food, local transportation, and sightseeing.

All of these average travel rates were compiled from prior travelers to help you plan your trip budget.

A one-week trip to Tennessee costs around $1,205 for one person and $2,409 for two. This includes accommodations, food, local transportation, and sightseeing.

A two-week trip to Tennessee will cost around $2,409 for one person and $4,819 for two. This fee includes hotel, food, local transportation, and sightseeing.

Please bear in mind that costs may differ based on your travel style, pace, and other considerations. Traveling as a family of three or four people often reduces the cost per person because children's tickets are less expensive and hotel rooms may be shared. If you go slower and for a longer amount of time, your daily budget will be reduced. Two people visiting Nashville for a month will almost always have a lower daily budget per person than one person visiting for a week.

A month in Tennessee costs about $5,163 for one individual and $10,325 for two. Because of increased transportation costs, the day charge rises as you visit more places

Chapter 3

How to Navigate Tennessee

When you get to Tennessee, you'll be wondering how to get around. I strongly advise you to rent a car at the airport for your trip.

BNA, like other major airports, provides a plethora of transportation options to and from the terminal.

Nashville's MTA bus system, for example, serves both arriving and outgoing passengers and has a variety of stops and drop-off places. Visit the MTA website for further information.

Various taxi companies also operate at the airport, with prices starting at $7 and increasing by $2.10 per mile beyond that. For excursions to downtown Nashville or the Gaylord Opryland Hotel, a set cost of $25 is applied. Many hotels offer free shuttle service, and Lyft and Uber are also licensed to operate at Nashville International.

Accommodation In Tennessee

Vandyke Bed & Beverages: takes a unique approach to the restaurant-with-rooms idea. Eight elegant, adult-only rooms are perched above one of Nashville's hippest cocktail bars. Consider Scandi-inspired décor, a sunny rooftop patio, and accessibility to popular nightlife destinations. Before you go out, sip handmade drinks and nibble on light nibbles. For well-heeled couples or groups of friends.

Address: 105 S 11th St, Nashville, Tennessee, 37206, United States

The 404: in Nashville is the smaller sister hotel to The 404 Kitchen, which is well-known for its contemporary spin on classic European food. Sleek rooms have custom-built furnishings and original artworks, making them ideal for gourmet couples wishing to relax only seconds away from the restaurant's scrumptious cuisine. This is an intimate designer choice with only five rooms.

Address: 404 12th Avenue South, Nashville, Tennessee 37203. United States.

The Dwell Hotel: has 16 vivid rooms and suites with mid-century contemporary décor and eye-catching patterned wallpaper. Choose this spot for a unique and private Chattanooga experience, replete with fantastic cuisine and creative beverages. Suitable for couples or groups of friends.

The Oliver.. is a modern boutique hotel in Knoxville with 28 clever rooms hidden behind a red-brick Victorian façade. Choose this location for the cool speakeasy bar, trendy restaurant, and convenient downtown location. A tiny, unique option for well-heeled couples or friends.

Address: 120 E. 10th Street Chattanooga, TN 37402

12Hotel: With 16 rooms with cast iron beds and monochromatic décor, the 121 Hotel in Nashville provides a luxury base for couples. Well-designed public rooms are ideal for gatherings or group retreats, but the atmosphere also appeals to young couples. Gourmet breakfasts are fantastic.

Address: 918 Knox Ave. Nashville, TN 37204.

Downtown Sporting Club: is a trendy Nashville hotel with only 20 rooms, some of which feature bunk beds for budget-conscious friends traveling together. In the famous restaurant, dine on American favorites, try your hand at axe-throwing, and visit the sports bar. A memorable city stay.

Address: **411 Broadway, Nashville, Tennessee 37203.**

Recommended Things To Do In Tennessee

1. Nashville: Hop-on Hop-off Trolley Tour

A hop-on hop-off trolley trip takes you around the highlights of Nashville, the "Home of Country Music." Pass through 'The District,' a downtown district with world-class shopping, restaurants, and entertainment. Discover Nashville's fascinating past. Take the Old Town Trolley to see popular sights such as the Country Music Hall of Fame and Museum, the Parthenon, and the Bicentennial Capitol Mall. It's more than simply a sightseeing trip; your trolley conductor gives an interesting commentary that contains little-known information, behind-the-scenes advice, and video clips. Avoid city traffic and expensive parking by choosing an option that allows you to focus on seeing the sites. When you're done, simply board the next Old Town Trolley to continue seeing everything Nashville has to offer. The Old Town Trolley, which combines transportation and entertainment, is the greatest way to experience the city. There are 13 useful stations available: 1) Marathon Motor Works, 1200 Clinton St. 2) North 27th Avenue: Centennial Park, The Parthenon 3) Hot Chicken at 1901 Broadway 4) Belmont Mansion, 1900 Belmont Blvd 5) The Gulch, 404 12th Ave. S. 6) Frist Art Museum, Union Station Hotel, 1037 Broadway 7) Country Music Hall of Fame, 472 Domonbreun St. 8) 201 Broadway: Bars with Live Music 9) Ryman Auditorium, 116 Rep. John Lewis Way 10) Legislative Plaza, State Capitol, 6th & Deadrick 11) Musicians Hall of Fame, 401 Gay St. 7th Avenue North: Farmers' Market Capitol View, 1018 Nelson Merry Street

2. Pigeon Forge: Titanic Museum Advance Purchase Ticket

Step aboard the famous Titanic Museum in Pigeon Forge to see the world's biggest collection of Titanic relics and interact with displays that appeal to people of all ages.

Listen to an audio tour that tells the narrative of the Titanic. Enter the Museum through a half-scale replica of the Titanic's exterior. Get your passenger boarding pass with the name of a Titanic passenger or crew member. Follow them throughout the ship, enter the Memorial Room, and learn what happened to your allocated individual. Admire the great staircase, which is worth a million dollars. Feel an iceberg, shovel "coal" in the Titanic's Boiler Room, and discover how to transmit an SOS distress signal. Participate as a family in this living classroom's hands-on opportunity to encourage, educate, and inspire. Every child receives a boarding permit featuring a youngster who sailed on the Titanic and may listen to a unique audio tour designed specifically for children. Don't forget about the onboard scavenger quest. New in 2023: The Titanic Museum pays tribute to the 135 children onboard the RMS Titanic, who ranged in age from 9 weeks to 15 years and each had a unique tale to share. New exhibits. There are new stories. At this moment, all visitors can pay respect to these young lives.

3. Nashville: Grand Ole Opry Show Ticket

Visit the Grand Ole Opry House, Country Music's most iconic stage, to round out your trip to Music City. Every week, this renowned live performance and radio broadcast brings together emerging artists, superstars, and country classics on stage, along with bluegrass, family-friendly comedy, and more. Opry concerts are never rehearsed, and no two shows are ever the same. In one night, you will be taken on a musical trip through the various shades of Country, Western, and Americana music. This is a must-see event for enthusiasts of all ages. Choose your seating location when you buy and enjoy a wonderful evening at the Grand Ole Opry. Choose a Premium Experience option to upgrade your visit, which includes a concert ticket in either a Tier 1 or Tier 2 seat and admission to the exclusive Circle Room Lounge. You will meet an Opry performer, enjoy snacks, two premium drinks, and a souvenir snapshot to take home. Opens one hour before the show and stays open until intermission.

4. Country Music Hall of Fame and Museum in Nashville

The Country Music Hall of Fame and Museum tells the dramatic tale of one of the most significant innovations in twentieth-century American music. Enter the museum's central exhibition, Sing Me Back Home: A Journey Through Country Music, after passing through the grandiose Hall of Fame rotunda, which is modeled by musical notations and the black keys of a piano. Immerse yourself with the history and sounds of country music, as well as its roots and customs, as well as the stories and voices of many of its legendary architects. As you go around the museum's collection, you'll see a variety of images, objects, text panels, recordings, and historical films. Don't miss out on limited-time exhibitions highlighting the exciting period of country music in the 1970s, as well as digitally upgraded presentations concentrating on modern developments in the genre. On weekends, visit the Taylor Swift Education Center to participate in instrument and songwriting sessions or to attend a panel discussion. The museum tour culminates in the prestigious Hall of Fame Rotunda, where you can see the musicians' plaques who have received Country Music's greatest accolade. To go behind the scenes at Hatch Show Print, upgrade to the Hatch Experience. Discover the history of this legendary letterpress poster shop. Listen to the press churn and view 150 years of vividly colored posters for your favorite acts. Print your memento poster using the tools of the trade!

5. The Double-Decker City Tour in Nashville

On a double-decker tour bus, you can see the best of Music City. Your guide will take you on a loop around the center of Nashville, highlighting some of the city's top highlights. Take a double-decker bus tour around the city's most visually intriguing places in only one hour, making it ideal for hectic schedules. This journey, which includes over 100 areas of interest, is escorted by entertaining and knowledgeable drivers and experts. Begin your trip in the Court of Flags and work your way around Nissan Stadium and up to the Parthenon at

Centennial Park. It then returns to the State Capitol and proceeds down Lower Broadway. Along the route, see the Country Music Hall of Fame and Vanderbilt University, both of which are stately and majestic. You'll also come across a vibrant farmers market and the Grammy Museum Gallery.

6. <u>Skip-the-Line Admission Ticket to the Nashville Zoo</u>

With this Nashville Zoo at Grassmere entrance ticket, you may avoid long waits. Come prepared to enjoy the animals, activities, and eateries right away, without the hassle of in-person ticket purchasing and long wait periods. Learn about many creatures from across the world as you observe Tigers, Giraffes, Bears, Monkeys, Rhinos, Leopards, Flamingos, Turtles, and other species living in stunningly natural outdoor habitats along shaded walkways. Access to amphitheater animal performances, keeper talks, Critter Encounters, the Grassmere Historic Home, and other instructive and enjoyable activities are available. Take a break at one of the many restaurants and bars, and park easily in the available parking garage.

7. <u>Line Dancing Class in Nashville with Keepsake Video</u>

Feel like a line-dancing rockstar with a class that is enjoyable for both children and adults. Keep current with all of Nashville's country music songs by learning the most popular routines step by step. Work up to a full-length group choreography by following your teacher at a leisurely pace. Begin by having a casual meet-and-greet with your group and teacher to get to know one another. A short line dance follows to get everyone warmed up and ready to go. Your instructor will demonstrate three dances, and you will be able to pick which choreographies you wish to rehearse and master as a group. In the one-hour lesson, you'll learn back-to-back line dances that are popular in dance halls around the country. Take your time getting acquainted with and developing confidence with routines ranging from beginner to expert, depending on your experience and preferences. Don't forget to take a video of your dances at the end of the energetic session to show off your accomplishments to everyone at home.

8. <u>Nashville: Music City Night Tour</u>

Ride a stadium seating trolley across the city at night and hear amazing information about the city's musical history from your performing guide, who will play musical excerpts, sing along, and may even play a musical instrument. Learn intimate anecdotes and fascinating facts about Nashville's musical history. Investigate the city's contemporary music scene. Learn about the people, places, and events that helped Nashville acquire the moniker "Music City." The trolley tour passes many points of interest, such as the many recording studios on Music Row, the Ryman Auditorium, the Parthenon, the honky tonk bars on Broadway, the Musicians Hall of Fame, and the Tennessee State Capitol. Learn about the city's rhythm and blues heritage, honky tonks, and famous music venues. Discover the personalities that helped shape

Nashville's legendary music culture while taking in the sights of this dynamic city.

9. <u>Nashville: Stars' Homes Narrated Bus Tour</u>

Nashville is recognized as America's music capital, and this trip will take you to the homes of the city's top stars. View the lavish residences of celebrities such as Taylor Swift, Kellie Pickler, Joe Don Rooney of Rascal Flatts, Little Big Town, Martina McBride, Reese Witherspoon, and Dierks Bentley. I'm hoping that one of Nashville's music scene's luminaries will join on board, as they have in the past. On this unforgettable trip, you'll discover why so many celebrities call Nashville home and how it became America's music capital.

10. <u>Nashville: Combo of RCA Studio B and Country Music Hall of Fame</u>

Step back in time to share a room with your favorite performers and explore behind the scenes of some of country music's most legendary recording sessions.

Check-in at the Country Music Hall of Fame and Museum to receive your RCA Studio B tour slot. Board a vehicle with your tour guide and learn about Dolly's "first big break," a tragic Christmas recording session with Elvis, and much more. As famous songs play over the speakers, stand in the room and enjoy the enchantment. After your guided tour of the studio, board the bus to return to the Country Music Hall of Fame and Museum, where you may have a self-guided tour of one of the most significant breakthroughs in twentieth-century American music. Before entering the museum's main exhibition, Sing Me Back Home: A Journey Through Country Music, pass through the magnificent Hall of Fame rotunda, which is patterned after musical notations and the black keys of a piano. Immerse yourself with the history and sounds of country music, as well as its roots and customs, as well as the stories and voices of many of its legendary architects. As you go around the museum's collection, you'll come across a variety of images, objects, text panels, recordings, and historical films. Don't miss out on limited-time exhibitions highlighting the exciting period of country music in the 1970s, as well as digitally upgraded presentations concentrating on modern developments in the genre. On weekends, visit the Taylor Swift Education Center to participate in instrument and songwriting sessions or to attend a panel discussion. The tour of the museum culminates in the prestigious Hall of Fame Rotunda, where you can see the musicians' plaques who have received Country Music's greatest accolade. The entire family will leave with renewed enthusiasm and admiration for the talent of the legendary musicians who have made Nashville famous.

Top Rated Tourist Attractions in Tennessee

If you think the most frequented national parks in the United States are the Grand Canyon, Yellowstone, or Yosemite, you've probably never been to Tennessee. You might be shocked to find that the most visited national park in the United States is, in fact, the Great Smoky Mountains, also known as the "Smokies."

This region of extraordinary natural beauty in the "Volunteer State" attracts approximately three times the number of visitors as the Grand Canyon. Tennessee's appeal stems in large part from its proximity to eight other states. It also has a lot to do with its breathtaking natural beauty, rich history, and world-class attractions.

Then there's the music. Tennessee was the birthplace of many of America's greatest musicians and musical genres, from Elvis Presley's rock 'n' roll legacy to country singers like Johnny Cash. With our list of top tourist attractions in Tennessee, you may discover the greatest scenic and music-related places, as well as Civil War sites and national landmarks.

1. The Smoky Mountains: Great Smoky Mountains National Park

The Great Smoky Mountains National Park is a unique Tennessee destination that combines adventure with world-class splendor. You can simply travel to the park's most popular locations to see and activities to do from downtown Gatlinburg. Another alternative is to take the chairlift to the slopes at Ober Gatlinburg, a ski resort and entertainment park that has events all year.

Drive to the Top of Old Smoky—6,643-foot-high Clingmans Dome—and make the short, steep slope to the Observation Tower for 360-degree vistas. The ideal season to visit the Smoky Mountains for hiking and sightseeing is from spring to fall, with winter a close second.

Aside from gorgeous driving, the park has other features.

2. <u>Graceland in Memphis</u>

Graceland is one of the most popular sights in Memphis, rivaling the White House in Washington, D.C. Graceland Mansion, the most renowned rock 'n' roll mansion in the world, is a destination for fans from all over the world. Tours of this beautiful stately mansion give insight into the life of Elvis Presley, the King of Rock 'n' Roll. Much of the property remains the same or has been restored to, the way it was when Elvis died at Graceland in 1977.

Elvis Presley's Memphis is a large warehouse-style structure with exhibitions and displays. You'll be amazed by his colorful clothes and learn about the forces that shaped his remarkable ascent to popularity. Check out the family mausoleum, which has moved admirers to tears. View an astounding collection of Elvis automobiles, planes, and memorabilia. Explore his living accommodations, which include the music room, TV room, and Jungle Den.

Several trip packages are available, including lodging at the opulent The Guest House at Graceland. Many exciting interactive displays and online tours are available on the Graceland website for anyone interested in a virtual visit.

Address: 3717 Elvis Presley Boulevard, Memphis, Tennessee

3. <u>Dollywood in Pigeon Forge</u>

Dollywood, named for country singer Dolly Parton (who owns the park), has long been Tennessee's most popular ticketed attraction, attracting over three million people each year. This booming 160-acre theme park, one of

Pigeon Forge's top attractions, delivers family enjoyment with its blend of folksy Smoky Mountains customs and crafts, exhilarating rides, and musical entertainment.

Dollywood boasts more than 50 rides scattered over 11 themed zones, nine of which are roller coasters, including the iconic Tennessee Tornado. Timber Canyon, Country Fair, and Jukebox Junction are examples of east Tennessee culture and heritage.

Other attractions include live concerts, festivals, and the Dollywood Express, an actual coal-fired steam train that encircle the park. Make a day of it by include Splash Country.

Remember that Dollywood is closed from January to mid-March in order to prepare for the upcoming season, so plan your visit appropriately.

Address: 2700 Dollywood Parks Boulevard, Pigeon Forge, Tennessee

4. <u>Nashville: Music City USA</u>

Tennessee has a rich musical tapestry that no other American state can match. The Grand Ole Opry House and the Ryman Auditorium are two significant music-related sites in Nashville. The Union Gospel Tabernacle, which was established in 1892, is widely regarded as the Mother Church of Country Music. The first Opry, as well as the location for live radio broadcasts, was responsible for putting the Opry on the musical map.

The Country Music Hall of Fame and Museum, as well as granite stars placed on the pavement across the street, honor prominent country music celebrities. These sights are easily accessible by foot from the Ryman.

Take the Hall of fame tour, which includes a stop at RCA's Studio B on Music Row and the excitement of standing where Elvis Presley, Dolly Parton, and Willie Nelson recorded. Walk the "music mile" down Music

Row to observe the country music industry's headquarters.

Nashville's other musical attractions include the Johnny Cash Museum, Glen Campbell Museum and Rhinestone Stage, Gallery of Iconic Guitars at Belmont, and Musicians Hall of Fame and Museum.

5. <u>Home of the Blues: Memphis</u>

Beale Street in downtown Memphis is the birthplace of blues music. Elvis Presley, B.B. King, and Memphis Minnie all received their big break as entertainers on this famous historic street. The Memphis Music Hall of Fame, the Smithsonian's Memphis Rock 'n' Soul Museum, and the WC Handy Home and Museum, a monument to the Father of the Blues, are among the highlights in and near Beale Street.

Add the STAX Museum of American Soul, with its facsimile of the old Stax Records studio, to your must-see list of Memphis's most iconic music attractions.

Sun Studio, recognized as the birthplace of rock 'n' roll, is another historic landmark. Your tour guide will tell you stories of Elvis Presley, Jerry Lee Lewis, B.B. King, and Roy Orbison, all of whom were recorded here. This is where Elvis, at the age of 18, allegedly informed music producer Sam Phillips, "I don't sound like nobody."

6. <u>The Titanic Museum, Pigeon Forge</u>

The Titanic Museum in Pigeon Forge, Tennessee, brings to life a treasure mine of memories and memorabilia from the RMS Titanic—the world's largest of its sort. When you enter the museum, you feel as if you're aboard the actual ship; it's created in the design of the ship, but at half the scale.

Highlights include around 400 Titanic-related objects displayed in 20 galleries meant to make you feel like you're truly aboard the ship. Self-guided tours last around two hours. Following the events of the Titanic in chronological sequence, you will learn about the ship's design and the 10,000 talented artisans and laborers that built her. View rare photographs of the Titanic setting sail on its fateful maiden voyage.

Address: Pigeon Forge, Tennessee, 2134 Parkway.

7. Memphis's National Civil Rights Museum is number seven.

The National Civil Rights Museum in Memphis is a national treasure and one of Tennessee's most captivating attractions. The museum houses hundreds of objects dispersed across two buildings, including the Lorraine Motel, where Martin Luther King Jr. was slain in April 1968.

Stand in the room where assassin James Earl Ray squeezed the trigger that killed Martin Luther King Jr. Your attention will be drawn to the history of these momentous days, including motivating philosophies. View on-display artifacts and 40 short movies, oral narratives, and interactive media. Spend at least two to three hours visiting this attraction.

Your self-guided tour of the museum includes slavery, reconstruction after the Civil War, Jim Crow segregation, the 1950s Birmingham bus boycott Rosa Parks protest, and 1960s marches and sit-ins. The museum is instructive, inspiring, and a constant reminder of the need for racial equality.

Address: Memphis, Tennessee, 450 Mulberry Street

8. <u>Chattanooga's Tennessee Aquarium</u>

For 30 years, the Tennessee Aquarium has been educating visitors about aquatic organisms and habitats. The aquarium, located on the banks of the Tennessee River, immerses you in two experiences: River Journey and Ocean Journey. These riparian and marine environments are housed in massive tanks, the largest of which holds 618,000 gallons. The Tennessee Aquarium is the state's biggest, with over 800 species.

Visitors are engaged in hands-on learning by staff. Feeling the backs of stingrays as they glide by you in open touch tanks will either excite or repulse you.

Submerged scuba divers divert your attention to bright fish and massive octopuses. Whether you are drawn to the river or the sea, the Tennessee Aquarium is guaranteed to pique your interest in these enchanting ecosystems.

Address: 1 Broad Street, Chattanooga, Tennessee

9. **The Andrew Jackson Hermitage**

Andrew Jackson's Hermitage, the plantation residence of the seventh US President from 1804 until 1845, lies just a few miles east of Nashville. The present residence, which was erected in 1819, not long before Jackson was elected president, is well worth the couple of hours it takes to visit.

The park-like grounds and forests, as well as the mausoleum where both Jackson and his wife were put to rest, are highlights. The home was one of the country's first presidential museums when it debuted as a museum in 1889. After extensive restoration, it now seems to be precisely as it was during Jackson's retirement, complete with countless artifacts and papers connected to his administration.

Address: 4580 Rachel's Lane in Nashville, Tennessee

10. <u>Lookout Mountain near Chattanooga</u>

Lookout Mountain, which overlooks Chattanooga and has some of Tennessee's greatest vistas, is a great day or half-day excursion. Natural features in Georgia include the gardens and High Falls in Rock City, as well as Ruby Falls, the highest and deepest accessible subterranean waterfall in the United States.

When you ride the Lookout Mountain inclination Railway, a mile-long excursion on a trolley-style car that goes up an inclination of up to 73 percent, getting to Lookout Mountain might be half the pleasure.

Once at the top of the railway, the Chickamauga-Chattanooga National Military Park's Point Park Battlefield lies close. Battles for Chattanooga Electric Map and Museum is a must-see. Its exhibits are based on the epic Battle Above the Clouds, which took place in and near Chattanooga during the Civil War.

11. <u>The Civil War Heritage of Tennessee</u>

Tennessee, the final state to join the Confederacy, was torn throughout the Civil War. The west and midsection of the state-supported Confederate forces, while the east supported Union troops.

Tennessee, being one of the Confederacy's northernmost states, saw multiple conflicts throughout the four-year struggle, many of which are preserved by tourist centers, museums, cemeteries, and memorials.

Fort Donelson National Battlefield is home to a cemetery, fort, and tourist center, as well as one of the first important Union triumphs. Shiloh National Military Park encompasses 6,000 acres on the location of the 1862 two-day fight. Shiloh was the site of the first big Civil War engagement in the Western Theater, and it now has a cemetery with about 3,500 Union graves.

The country's largest military park, Chickamauga-Chattanooga National Military Park, was historically significant in the Civil War. The fight that signified the fall of the Confederacy took place in the 9,500-acre park.

12. Knoxville's Downtown

Knoxville is a convenient location for touring and exploring the Great Smoky Mountains National Park. The Sunsphere is the most visible feature in the state's initial capital. The Sunsphere, a symbol of Knoxville's skyline, is located in the middle of the 1982 World's Fair Park. The observation deck on the fourth level offers spectacular 360-degree views of downtown Knoxville and the mountains.

The Museum of East Tennessee History, located on vibrant South Gay Street, features interactive displays. The magnificent Tennessee Theatre—the Official State Theatre of Tennessee—is also where you can witness big concerts and Broadway-style productions. It was deemed "the South's most beautiful theater" when it was opened in October 1928.

Market Square, one block west of Gay Street, has been Knoxville's favorite meeting area since 1854. It now hosts a bustling farmers' market, events, and festivals, as well as shopping and dining. Krutch Park, adjacent to the square, is a tranquil green spot for rest and appreciation of contemporary pieces of public art.

13. <u>Chattanooga and the Tennessee Valley Railroad</u>

Tennessee has a long history with the railroad. The Southern Confederate Army relied on railways to convey military supplies during the Civil War. Railways and waterways were critical for delivering timber and cotton during peacetime.

Tennessee's significant railway legacy has been preserved across the state. The station and an engine from the legendary Chattanooga Choo Choo are the most remarkable remains. Visit the museum devoted to the great railroad engineer, John Luther "Casey" Jones, in Jackson.

The Tennessee Valley Railroad, or TVR, is one of the most complex rehabilitation efforts. The TVR provides tourist trips in the Chattanooga region and along the Hiwassee River in the Smoky Mountains. The Three Rivers Rambler in Knoxville takes you 11 miles along three rivers, including the Tennessee, on a vintage coal-fired steam engine locomotive. Take advantage of the ride-and-dine packages available on certain trains.

14. <u>Nashville's The Parthenon</u>

No trip to Nashville would be complete without a stop at the massive Parthenon. It is the centerpiece of Centennial Park, a short walk from the city's central core, and is one of Tennessee's most stunning sights. This amazing life-size copy of the real Parthenon in Athens, Greece, took ten years to build and opened in 1931.

The Parthenon, built of brick, stone, and concrete, is impressive both inside and out. The structure holds the city's permanent art gallery, a collection of paintings by 19th and 20th-century American painters, and a magnificent 42-foot gold-covered statue of the goddess Athena Parthenos. The Parthenon is included on the National Historic Register.

Address: Nashville, Tennessee 2500 West End Avenue

15. American Museum of Science and Energy, Oak Ridge

The American Museum of Science and Energy in Oak Ridge provides an intriguing look at the history of nuclear energy. The museum, which is located 24 miles west of Knoxville, honors Oak Ridge's pivotal role in the Manhattan Project's development of the first atomic weapon.

Explore this massive institution through movies, images, relics, and papers. Discover how it grew throughout time to become a key hub for scientific study and innovation. Visitors of all ages are entertained by interactive exhibits of static electricity and robotics.

Address 115 East Main Street, Oak Ridge, Tennessee.

16. <u>The Museum of Appalachia</u>

The Museum of Appalachia, one of the greatest heritage towns in the United States, is a major open-air attraction that focuses on the people who populated the Appalachian Mountains. The museum allows you to learn about the past by doing hands-on activities like weaving and farming. You'll leave with a better understanding of mountain culture, livelihoods, and customs.

The Museum of Appalachia, with over 250,000 relics dispersed around 65 pastoral acres, lies 6.6 miles north of Clinton, one of Tennessee's greatest little towns. You'll find an outstanding selection of baskets, home furnishings, musical instruments, folk art, and agricultural machinery.

If you become hungry, the museum's restaurant serves Southern Appalachian country food.

Address: 2819 Andersonville Hwy, Clinton, Tennesse

Tennessee Outdoor Experiences: The

state of Tennessee has a plethora of fantastic outdoor experiences. Those interested in fly fishing will find plenty of options in Tennessee, owing to the state's 22,000-plus miles of streams and reservoirs. Hikers, cyclists, campers, and skiers are among the numerous outdoor enthusiasts who visit Great Smoky Mountains National Park because there is so much wilderness to explore.

Tourist Attractions Close to Tennessee: Kentucky, located to the north of Tennessee, has several attractions and areas of interest worth visiting. The Kentucky Derby and The Kentucky Horse Park are must-sees, as are beautiful natural sights like

Cumberland Gap National Historical Park and Daniel Boone National Forest.

Tennessee's Bars and Pubs With Best Spots

You're in luck if you're searching for a night out on the town in East Tennessee. This area has a thriving and diversified nightlife scene with something for everyone. You'll find everything here, whether you're looking for artisan beer, live music, or high-energy dance clubs. In this post, we'll look at some of the top East Tennessee pubs, clubs, and entertainment places.

- ## Exploring the Exciting Nightlife Scene in East Tennessee

The attractiveness of East Tennessee's nightlife is one of its distinguishing features. Each place, from tiny pubs to upmarket nightclubs, has its personality and vibe. No matter where you go, you'll encounter nice locals and a pleasant atmosphere.

• The Allure of East Tennessee's Nightlife

You don't have to spend a fortune on a night out in East Tennessee. Many of the area's nightclubs and clubs have reasonable drink and food rates. If you enjoy live music, you'll be pleased to learn that various locations host local performers and bands. If you're looking for something a little more low-key, there are plenty of charming pubs and wine bars to choose from.

The range of places offered is one of the finest aspects of East Tennessee's nightlife. You'll find everything here, from a busy dance club to a peaceful wine bar. And with so many possibilities, you're bound to find a new favorite location every time you go out.

East Tennessee's nightlife culture is noted for its friendly residents, in addition to its wonderful atmosphere and range of places. Whether you're a native or simply passing through, you'll feel perfectly at home in any of the neighborhood's pubs or clubs. And with so many nice people around, you're bound to meet new people and have a good time.

• East Tennessee's Most Popular Nightlife

East Tennessee's most popular nightlife cities include Knoxville, Chattanooga, and Gatlinburg. There are several pubs, clubs, and entertainment places to select from in these cities. Whether you want a high-energy dance club or a laid-back bar, you'll find it here.

Knoxville is well-known for its lively downtown district, which is home to a plethora of pubs and clubs. In this lively city, you can find everything from sophisticated cocktail lounges to dive bars. With a strong local music culture, you're bound to catch a wonderful live act while out and about.

Chattanooga is another wonderful nightlife destination in East Tennessee. Several notable nightclubs and clubs, as well as a range of restaurants and stores, can be found in the city's Southside sector. And, with wonderful views of the Tennessee River, you may enjoy a lovely backdrop while out on the town.

Gatlinburg is an excellent choice for a more relaxed nighttime experience. This little mountain village has several snug taverns and wine bars, as well as several family-friendly attractions. And, because of its closeness to the Great Smoky Mountains National Park, you can take in some of the most breathtaking scenery in the country while you're out and about.

- ## Top East Tennessee Bars and Pubs

If you enjoy artisan beer, whiskey, wine, or simply nice company, East Tennessee has plenty to offer. This dynamic region of the United States has something for everyone, from sports bars to craft beer destinations. Here are some of the best local bars and pubs:

• Craft Beer Hotspots

East Tennessee has several craft breweries and beer pubs. The Casual Pint, The Public House, and Last Days of Autumn Brewing are among the best places to have a cool one. These establishments provide a range of locally made beers and ales, as well as great bar food. You may enjoy a pint of your favorite beer while playing cornhole with pals at the Casual Pint. The Public House, on the other hand, is recognized for its comfortable setting and friendly staff who are always willing to offer a new beer to sample. Last Days of Autumn Brewing is ideal for individuals who enjoy IPAs and stouts, as well as a changing collection of seasonal brews that are guaranteed to delight.

• Bourbon and Whiskey Bars

East Tennessee has plenty of whiskey and bourbon alternatives for whiskey and bourbon enthusiasts. Bourbon, whiskey, and other spirits are available at Old City Wine Bar, Suttree's High Gravity Tavern, and Merchants of Beer. These establishments also have educated bartenders who can propose the ideal drink for you. You may have a drink of bourbon while listening to live music on the outside terrace at Old City Wine Bar. Suttree's High Gravity Tavern is well-known for its vast collection of rare and difficult-to-find whiskeys, whilst Merchants of Beer is ideal for individuals who enjoy tasting new and distinctive craft brews.

• Tasting Rooms and Wine Bars

If you're in the mood for a glass of wine, East Tennessee has much to offer. Wine tastings and pairings are available at Blue Slip Winery, Corks Wine and Spirits, and Ember's Tavern & Grille, among other locations. Blue Slip Winery is an excellent place to sip a bottle of wine while admiring the breathtaking views of the Tennessee River. Corks Wine and Spirits, on the other hand, is noted for its expert staff that can assist you in selecting the ideal wine to complement your dinner. Ember's Tavern and Grille is a welcoming establishment that serves a wide selection of reds, whites, and sparkling wines, as well as craft beers and cocktails.

• Taverns and Sports Bars

If you enjoy sports, you'll enjoy East Tennessee's collection of sports pubs and taverns. Sports bars and restaurants such as Buffalo Wild Wings, Wild Wing Cafe, and Scoreboard Sports Bar & Grill provide plenty of TVs and a vibrant atmosphere for viewing the game. You may enjoy a dish of hot wings while rooting for your favorite team at Buffalo Wild Wings. The Wild Wing Cafe is well-known for its vast beer menu and live music events, whilst Scoreboard Sports Bar & Grill is a terrific place to watch a game while eating a burger and fries.

• Specialty and themed bars

If you're looking for something out of the ordinary, East Tennessee has a plethora of themed and specialty pubs to select from. Preservation Pub, Latitude 35, and The Peter Kern Library all have distinct atmospheres and creative drinks that will transport you to another era and location.

Preservation Pub is a quaint hangout with live music and a changing menu of artisan beers and beverages. Latitude 35 is a tiki-themed bar that serves tropical beverages and delectable small meals. The Peter Kern Library is a speakeasy-style bar concealed behind a bookcase that serves traditional drinks in a pleasant, private setting.

• East Tennessee's Best Nightclubs and Dance Clubs

If you want to spend the night dancing and having a good time, East Tennessee provides lots of possibilities for you. There's something for everyone, from high-energy dance clubs to private and expensive establishments. Here are some of the greatest local nightclubs and dance clubs:

• High-Intensity Dance Clubs

For those who enjoy dancing the night away, venues such as NV Nightclub, The Edge, and New Amsterdam provide high-energy dance floors and thundering music.

With a large dance floor and a range of drink deals, The Edge in downtown Knoxville is a favorite hangout for college students and young professionals. The NV Nightclub, located in the center of Chattanooga, is recognized for its cutting-edge sound system and spectacular light show. New Amsterdam, is a fashionable place in Nashville, with a rooftop bar and a variety of themed events, including 80s and 90s dance parties.

Nightclubs Accepting LGBTQ+ People

East Tennessee also has several LGBTQ+-friendly nightclubs, such as Club XYZ in Knoxville and Alan Gold's in Nashville. These establishments provide a welcoming and comfortable environment for members of the LGBTQ+ community to gather and live free on the dance floor. Club XYZ, located in Knoxville's historic Old City area, is well-known for its drag acts and themed evenings, such as "RuPaul's Drag Race" viewing parties. Alan Gold's, located in Nashville's LGBT neighborhood, is a popular place for dancing and socializing, featuring a large dance floor and a range of drink deals.

Venues for Live Music and Performance

East Tennessee boasts a plethora of live music and performance venues for music fans to enjoy. The Bijou Theatre in downtown Knoxville is a historic facility that has featured several well-known performers and comedians throughout the years. The Signal in Chattanooga is a newer facility that has rapidly become a popular live music venue, thanks to its big dance floor and excellent sound quality. The Tennessee Theatre, also in downtown Knoxville, is a beautifully refurbished facility that plays a range of musical performers and Broadway productions all year.

Exclusive and Elegant Clubs

If you're looking for a more exclusive and affluent experience, East Tennessee provides a few possibilities for you. The Standard is a sleek and stylish downtown Knoxville venue that provides VIP bottle service and a choice of specialty drinks. With a sophisticated setting and a variety of themed events, The Social in Chattanooga is a favorite destination for young professionals and celebrities. Lounge 9 in Nashville is a hip hangout with a rooftop bar and a menu of high-end drinks and spirits.

Whatever type of nightlife experience you seek, East Tennessee offers something for you. From high-energy dance clubs to private and premium settings, you're sure to find something to your liking.

If you want to do anything other than drink and dance, East Tennessee has some interesting entertainment places to check out:

- ## **Open Mic Nights and Comedy Clubs**

Stand-up comedy and open mic evenings are available at venues such as Side Splitters Comedy Club and Scruffy City Hall for individuals who like a good laugh. These venues frequently showcase local comedians as well as emerging talent from throughout the country.

Side Splitters Comedy Club has a pleasant setting as well as a complete bar and restaurant. The club is well-known for its humorous shows, which have included comedians such as Josh Blue and Colin Mochrie. In contrast, Scruffy City Hall is a rustic venue with a laid-back ambiance. Open mic evenings at the venue are a terrific way for budding comedians to test out their stuff.

• Karaoke and Sing-Along Venues

If you enjoy singing, East Tennessee boasts a plethora of karaoke bars and sing-along venues where you may showcase your abilities. Karaoke evenings and sing-along events are available at venues such as Southbound Knoxville, The Drake, and Birdhouse on the Greenway.

Southbound Knoxville is a country-themed pub that hosts karaoke nights on Thursdays. With its broad song selection and energetic environment, The Drake, located in the center of downtown Knoxville, is a favorite venue for karaoke and sing-alongs. With its outside terrace and fire pits, Birdhouse on the Greenway, located in a lovely old structure, provides a one-of-a-kind karaoke experience.

- **Gaming and arcade establishments**

If you enjoy video games and arcade oldies, East Tennessee offers great gaming and arcade bars for you. Token Game Tavern, Game On, and Level Up, for example, provide traditional arcade games, console games, and board games for guests to enjoy while drinking drinks.

Token Game Tavern in Knoxville is a popular hangout for both gamers and non-gamers. The pub has a complete bar and food menu, as well as a large range of board games, video games, and old arcade games. Game On, located in Johnson City, is a gaming pub with a friendly environment and a wide selection of console games. Level Up in Chattanooga is a throwback arcade bar that features classic games such as Pac-Man and Donkey Kong.

Outdoor and Rooftop Locations

Finally, for those who want to enjoy the evening beneath the stars, East Tennessee offers some lovely outdoor and rooftop places. Venues like The Rooftop at Ole Red, Pour Taproom, and Lonesome Dove Knoxville provide stunning vistas and a one-of-a-kind environment for a night out.

The Rooftop at Ole Red in Gatlinburg has breathtaking views of the Great Smoky Mountains as well as a vibrant ambiance with live music and a full bar. Pour Taproom in downtown Knoxville is a one-of-a-kind self-serve beer pub with an outside patio overlooking Market Square. The rooftop bar of Lonesome Dove Knoxville, located in the historic Old City, with a warm fireplace and views of downtown Knoxville.

Tennessee Dining and Cuisine With Best Spots

Tennessee's most famous dish is likely country ham. The hams are salt-cured and offered boiled, grilled, or fried, and they compete with Virginia's Smithfield hams.

Nashville is a culinary gem famed for its meat-and-three eateries, spicy fried chicken, and fluffy biscuits, as well as a thriving farm-to-table culture. Eat like a local with our guide to some of Music City's top restaurants and bars.

What You Shouldn't Miss When Visiting Tennessee

- Hot Chicken. When we ate this spicy chicken at Pepperfire in Tennessee, we dropped it like it was hot...
- Biscuits. In Tennessee, biscuits come in a variety of forms and sizes...
- Meat and Three...
- Brunch...
- Chocolate...
- Donuts....
- Third Wave Coffee...
- Tennessee Whiskey.

Chapter 4

Check-out My Choicest Restaurants

Alleia

Alleia is located at 25 E. Main St. in Chattanooga;423-305-6990 alleiarestaurant.com. Daniel Lindley, a Chattanooga native who opened St. John's Restaurant in 2000 and has been nominated for a James Beard award six times, improves Scenic City's dining scene with his simple, Italian-inspired cooking at Alleia. More than a half-dozen housemade pasta, pizzas cooked in a 750-degree brick oven, and meals like bacon-wrapped quail breast ($24) or grouper with succotash ($28) are available.

Bastion

615-490-8434; bastionnashville.com; Bastion 434 Houston St., Nashville

Strategic Hospitality and chef Josh Habiger's Wedgewood-Houston hot spot combines two experiences in one: a laid-back, trendy bar with excellent cocktails and plates of gooey nachos ($10-12), and an intimate, 24-seat high-end restaurant with an inventive and constantly changing multi-course menu ($25 deposit per person required at time of reservation will be applied to your final bill).

Biscuit Love

Biscuit Love, 316 11th Avenue South, Nashville, 615-490-9584, biscuitlove.com

Don't be put off by the early-morning crowds at Biscuit Love, a food truck turned massively famous Nashville restaurant with two locations. The line goes quickly, and the wait is worth it. The East Nasty biscuit sandwich with fried chicken, aged cheddar, and sausage gravy ($10), and the Lindstrom, a shaved Brussel sprouts salad with hazelnuts, parmesan, and lemon vinaigrette topped with two poached eggs ($9), are all must-orders.

City House

615-736-5838; cityhousenashville.com; 1222 4th Ave. N., Nashville

Tandy Wilson, a James Beard Award winner, shines at his Germantown restaurant, where seasonal salads, delectable pasta, and imaginative thin-crust pizzas take center stage. Salad choices may appear basic, but they will impress your taste buds ($9-13), and don't miss the classic fatty ham pizza with a creamy fried egg on top ($17).

Hog & Hominy

707 W. Brookhaven Circle, Memphis; 901-207-7396; hogandhominy.com

Since its inception in 2012, Hog & Hominy has received several national distinctions. The restaurant successfully integrates Italian cooking with Southern traditions, resulting in delicious pizzas like the mushroom, smoked arugula, cream, and garlic pie ($16), as well as unusual dishes like the biscuit gnocchi with lamb pancetta, ramps, and morels ($15). After dinner, make a night of it by going to the bocce ball court.

J.C. Holdway

501 Union Avenue, Knoxville; 865-312-9050; jcholdway.com

At his J.C. Holdway restaurant, Knoxville native chef Joseph Lenn uses wood-fired cooking techniques to pay homage to Appalachian food and Southern farmers. Smoked catfish onion dip and BBQ potato chips ($11), grilled bone marrow with charred broccoli salad, radish, and bread ($13), and wood-grilled pig with leeks, sea island red peas, tomatoes, and basil pistou ($25) are among the menu selections.

Prince's Hot Chicken Shack

615-226-9442; princeshotchicken.com; Prince's Hot Chicken Shack, 123 Ewing Drive #3 and 5814 Nolensville Road Suite 110, Nashville

As Nashville's dining industry evolves at a breakneck speed, luring TV chefs and James Beard Award winners from all over the country, Prince's Hot Chicken Shack has stayed loyal to its mission: to blow people's socks off with the tastiest hot chicken. The no-frills diner with two Nashville locations has spawned copycats as far away as Los Angeles ($5 for three whole wings with a slice of bread and pickles; $11 for a half chicken; $2 sides).

Restaurant Iris

Restaurant Iris is located at 2146 Monroe Avenue in Memphis and can be reached at 901-590-2828.

Chef Kelly English dazzles customers at Memphis' award-winning Restaurant Iris, which is housed in a charmingly refurbished mansion. A lobster knuckle sandwich with tarragon and tomatoes ($18), grilled lamb loin ($36), and pan-seared Alaskan halibut ($34) are among the items on the French-Creole-inspired menu. I

The Stock & Barrel is located at 35 Market Square in Knoxville and can be reached at 865-766-2075.

Burger restaurant in Knoxville The Stock & Barrel collaborates with Tennessee producers to create its delectable food. Mitchell Family Farms in Blaine, Tennessee, provides the beef, while Knoxville's own Flour Head Bakery provides the buns. The menu features 20 burgers, ranging from the conventional The 'Merican with American cheese, pickles, onions, tomato, greens, and mayo (10.5), to the inventive Elvis burger with organic peanut butter, fried bananas, and Benton's bacon ($11.5).

The Wild Plum Tea Room

The Wild Plum Tea Room is located at 555 Buckhorn Road in Gatlinburg and can be reached at 865-436-3808 or wildplumtearoom.com.

The Wild Plum, a tiny and quirky tea place off the main path in Gatlinburg, provides a refreshing lunch choice with attentive service. In the outside garden, have wild plum tea, housemade chicken salad with fresh fruit and a warm scone ($9.95), or lobster pie ($17.95) for a surreal experience.

Shopping And Leisure With Best Spots

Tennessee's retail opportunities are as diverse as its localities. In tourist areas like Gatlinburg's European Village and Pigeon Forge, it's all about knick-knack souvenirs and outlet stores. Pigeon Forge Factory Outlet

Mall offers nearly as many large-name shops as Belz Factory Outlet World. These two venues are popular with shoppers searching for substantial discounts on popular products.

Retailers in major cities like Memphis genuinely cover the complete spectrum. There are several gaudy Elvis souvenir shops on Beale Street and in the vicinity of Graceland, but there are also upscale merchants in East Memphis retail complexes and communities. There is no one shopping hub here, so you'll have to travel to enjoy the whole experience. South Main Historic District has recently been a trendy destination for offbeat boutiques, and antiques may be found on South Cooper Street and Central Avenue.

Nashville also has a great retail environment, but it is distributed around the city, blending modern shopping malls on the outskirts with historic downtown areas and its unique merchants. As befits a country western community, there are some beautiful western clothes boutiques in the District, Music Valley, and along Music Row. Another wonderful buy in Nashville is antiques, which can be found in stores around Douglas Street and Eighth Avenue South. In Nashville, souvenirs are quite popular, and it's never difficult to find a music store loaded with instruments and other related items. Music stores abound on Beale Street and throughout the downtown area.

Best Beaches in Tennessee To Visit

Although Tennessee isn't recognized for its beaches, it doesn't imply they don't exist. In reality, the state has numerous excellent alternatives for people seeking sun and sand.

Beach visits are fantastic in Tennessee; all you need to do is bring the appropriate beach gear and you're prepared for an excellent day.

BIG RIDGE LAKE

Every year, BIG RIDGE LAKE exposes its sandy beach to guests. Families that visit may participate in a variety of interesting activities in the neighborhood, such as beach volleyball, basketball, tennis, softball, and more!

There are more than 50 campsites and 20 cottages if you wish to stay for a night or two. There is plenty of space to swim and open tables for a good family meal.

Big Ridge Lake is a tiny lake in Union County, Tennessee, situated in Big Ridge State Park. The lake is surrounded by thick woodland and rolling hills, making it an idyllic location for swimming, fishing, and boating. We strongly advise you to include Big Ridge Lake on your list of Tennessee beaches to visit!

CORDELL HULL LAKE

Cordell Hull Lake is a significant reservoir in Tennessee's Upper Cumberland area. The lake is named after Cordell Hull, who was Secretary of State under President Franklin D. Roosevelt and was instrumental in the formation of the United Nations.

Cordell Hull Lake was developed by the United States Army Corps of Engineers and provides a variety of family-friendly activities.

This beach offers several recreational options such as boating, fishing, picnics, and more.

If you wish to camp for a night or two, check out the two nearby campgrounds, which offer over 150 campsites in total.

CHEROKEE LAKE

Cherokee Lake is a major reservoir in East Tennessee that stretches over Jefferson, Grainger, and Hawkins counties. The lake was formed by the construction of the Cherokee Dam on the Holston River, and it provides tourists with a variety of recreational opportunities.

Cherokee Lake is a famous site for bass fishing in the area. It's a terrific beach for campers, fishers, and paddlers alike, and it's surrounded by beautiful hills and farms. For those who want to remain, there are various boat docks and picnic places, as well as campers.

There are many activities surrounding Cherokee Lake, such as fireworks displays and parties, so make sure to check their local calendar. This location is stunning, and it is one of our favorite Tennessee beaches.

CHEATHAM LAKE

Cheatham Lake made our list of Tennessee's greatest beaches! It is a man-made lake near Ashland City, Tennessee, located in the Cheatham Dam. It is part of the Nashville District of the United States Army Corps of Engineers and is recognized for its recreational opportunities and natural beauty.

The lake provides a variety of outdoor activities, including boating, fishing, swimming, and camping, as well as hiking and picnics.

Families may enjoy more than 320 miles of coastline on Cheatham Lake. There are 18 boat ramps, 14 playgrounds, and two marinas on the shore. This area is fantastic for water activities like kayaking, wakeboarding, and water skiing and is ideal for families. The lake is stocked with species such as bass, catfish, and crappie, making it a popular fishing destination. Around the lake, there are various campgrounds, boat launches, fishing piers, and hiking routes that allow access to the lake and the natural beauty of the region.

CENTER HILL LAKE

The Collins and Caney Fork rivers combine to form Center Hill Lake. With 400 miles of beachfront, three historic houses, and two stunning waterfalls, this beautiful beach has a lot to offer. The Caney Fork River is ideal for fishing, boating, kayaking, and hiking, while Center Hill Lake is ideal for swimming and fishing. There are two campgrounds with a total of 60 campsites and 10 cottages.

CHICKAMAUGA LAKE

Chickamauga Lake was named after the Chickamauga Cherokee Tribe, who once lived on the property. Because of its 1,300 kilometers of beachfront, it is a very popular family getaway. In addition, the lake is surrounded by two wildlife centers, a museum, and eight parks. Paddleboarding, water skiing, swimming, fishing, and boating are some of the lake's most popular water sports.

THE GRUNDY LAKES

Some of the greatest historical sites and hiking trails may be found in the Grundy Lakes area. Gather your friends for a picnic by the sea or lay out your blankets to soak up the rays. With 30,485 acres, the neighboring state park encompasses four state counties and provides lots of opportunities for exploration. There are several options to enhance your beach day at Grundy Lakes, including forests, waterfalls, streams, and cliffs.

J. PERCY PRIEST LAKE

If you're planning a trip to Nashville, we highly recommend stopping by J. Percy Priest Lake. Wakeboarding, fishing, sailing, swimming, water skiing, horseback riding, biking, picnics, and wildlife viewing are all available near downtown Nashville. If you choose to spend the night, there are three campsites scattered throughout the 42 miles of beach.

The rustic playground in Bryant Cove will appeal to children, while adults will enjoy joining in on a game of pickup volleyball. This is one of Tennessee's greatest beaches!

KENTUCKY LAKE

Given its size, Kentucky Lake might nearly be mistaken for an ocean. The lake covers more than 160,300 acres, so there is plenty of space for group camping, fishing, and water activities.

Nearby campsites, natural paths, and historic sites dot the shoreline. Keep an eye on the event schedule if you want to be a part of one of the many yearly events.

DALE HOLLOW LAKE

Another project attributable to the US Army Corps of Engineers is the Dale Hollow Reservoir. There is plenty of space for the family to enjoy boating, fishing, swimming, and water activities on the Kentucky-Tennessee border. Campers and houseboaters frequent the peaceful yet gorgeous beach.

There is a small park near First Christian Church where children may play, as well as a putt-putt course near the Methodist Church.

ROCK ISLAND STATE PARK

Rock Island State Park is one of my favorite spots to visit. This park on the Caney Fork River has some of the nicest swimming beaches in the state.

There are several day-use spaces with picnic tables and grills, making it ideal for a family picnic or BBQ. During the summer months, the park also offers a designated swimming area with lifeguards on duty, so you can feel comfortable letting your children play around.

Pay A Visit To The Museums

Museums are one of the country's most significant institutions. They contextualize our history, helping visitors to better understand civilizations and themselves. Good museum exhibits inspire contemplation, develop ideas, and foster respect for those who have gone before. Museums are public gems in many towns and cities, and they frequently score high in visitor visits.

Tennessee's east side

Attractions in Pigeon Forge: Titanic Museum, Pigeon Forge

Inside the Titanic Museum Attraction in Pigeon Forge, you may learn even more about the Titanic and its terrible voyage. As you walk through each exhibit, you'll be given a card about a Titanic passenger that covers everything from how the ship functioned to the luxurious fittings offered to first-class passengers. Feel an iceberg, the chilly water as the ship sinks, and much more.

Clinton's Green McAdoo Cultural Center

You may learn about the Clinton 12's remarkable story as they campaigned for equal access to public education.

Step inside a 1950s classroom to experience life under Jim Crow rules. With life-size images and anecdotes, follow the historical account of the desegregation of Clinton High School, the first integration of a public high school in the South.

Tennessee Rugby

Is it possible to consider a whole municipality to be a museum? It may be when it is kept as well as Rugby, Tennessee is. This live Victorian hamlet was founded in the 1880s by British immigrants seeking to construct a Utopian society. Take a springtime tour to see inside the historic buildings and the South's first public library. Spend a weekend staying in one of the historic lodges and exploring the 10 hiking trails that wind through the region.

Limestone's David Crockett Birthplace State Park

Visit David Crockett Birthplace State Park in Limestone, Tennessee, to learn about the actual man behind the mythology. The park honors the great Tennesseean, pioneer, soldier, and politician with a model cabin, visitor center displays, native 18th-century real farmhouse, and other attractions. It's close to his father's Crockett Tavern Museum and the Cherokee National Forest in Morristown.

Tennessee's Middle Region

Murfreesboro's Cannonsburgh Village

See how pioneers lived through the interactive Cannonsburgh Village in Murfreesboro, which represents more than 100 years of early Tennessee life. Tour a museum, a caboose, a schoolhouse, a gristmill, a telephone operator's cottage, and other historic sites. Self-guided tours are completely free.

Tullahoma's Beechcraft Heritage Museum

Away, away, away! Aviation enthusiasts will enjoy visiting the Beechcraft Heritage Museum in Tullahoma. Walk through three hangars full of planes. The Walter Beech Hangar houses some of the first aircraft types.

Military planes, notably pre-World War II Twin Beech Model 18Ds, may be found in the Alton E. "Chuck" Cianchette Hangar. A Staggerwing, one of the first general aviation aircraft to be tested in a wind tunnel, is also on exhibit. Two of the oldest 1947 Bonanzas, the first Model 55 Baton, and the final Duke ever built are all on display in the Bost Hangar.

Clarksville Customs House Museum and Cultural Center

The Customs House Museum and Cultural Center in Clarksville is Tennessee's second-biggest general museum, with over 35,000 square feet of display space packed with science, history, and fine art exhibits. Kids will enjoy McGregor's Market and Kitchen, as well as the toddler area, which features the Bubble Cave and elaborate model trains. A cabin from the 1840s, a massive china collection, and an 1898-designed Federal Post Office add to the state's heritage.

A porcelain collection and an 1898-designed Federal Post Office add to the state's heritage.

Tennessee's West

Memphis Brooks Museum of Art

The Memphis Brooks Museum of Art in Memphis constantly has something fresh to see. Currently on show are photographs, paintings, lithographs, and other works. Self-taught African American artists' paintings, sculptures, and textiles from the museum's permanent collection take center stage today until May 10. Carroll Cloar's artwork is also on display to mark the museum's 100th anniversary. Wednesdays through Sundays are the days that the museum is open.

Memphis' Edge Motor Museum

Memphis' only auto museum, which features more than a dozen legendary American sports cars, is officially open. The first show covers vehicles from the postwar United States to the 1970s and beyond. Each vehicle is curated by the museum based on the historical and cultural tale it portrays. Not only are the attributes of each automobile similar, but so is what was going on around the globe at the time the vehicle was manufactured. Edge Motor Museum tells the story of some of the world's most famous automobiles.

Jackson's Casey Jones Home & Railroad Museum

The Casey Jones Home & Railroad Museum tells the story of the legendary Casey Jones, his life, and his legendary last train voyage. There are three real rail cars, an original engine Jones drove, Civil War-era relics, and information on Jackson, Tennessee's rich railroad heritage. Kids may even hop onboard a train and ring the bell, just like Jones. After walking through time, visit The Old Country Store for a southern-style buffet, ice cream at the reconstructed 1880s Ice Cream Parlor and Fudge Shoppe, or a fast snack at the Dixie Café of Jackson, which features take-out options and an 1880s lunch counter.

Chapter 5

Top Insider's Tips and Tricks For Tennessee

Currency And Money

Tennessee's currency is the US dollar (US$). Banknotes are available in denominations of $1, $5, $10, $20, $50, and $100. One US dollar is made up of 100 cents, including one, five, ten, and twenty-five-cent coins. Foreign currency may be exchanged at most big banks in tourist areas such as Memphis, Nashville, and Pigeon Forge. While credit cards are often accepted in tourist regions, in rural areas, cash is preferred. ATMs that accept international credit cards are becoming more common in major cities.

Language

Residents of Tennessee speak English with a unique Southern accent. Because they consider that quick, aggressive communication is demeaning, locals speak slowly and attentively.

Slang words to use when you travel to Tennessee:

Are you ready to immerse yourself in the sounds of the Volunteer State? Understanding some Tennessee slang when touring throughout the state may make you feel like a real Tennessean. These slang terms will help you blend in with the friendly people of Tennessee, whether you're strolling through Nashville's colorful streets, listening to blues in Memphis, or climbing the scenic trails of Tennessee's Great Smoky Mountains. To help you blend in and make the most of your holiday, here are some slang words and phrases I picked up while there, as well as several handy websites:

1. "Y'all" - Let's start with the basics. "Y'all" is the cornerstone of Southern dialect. It's a friendly and inclusive way to address a group of people. "How y'all doin' today?"

2. "Bless Your Heart" - This phrase might sound sweet, but it can carry different meanings depending on the context. It's often used to express sympathy or understanding, but in some cases, it can be a polite way to say someone's made a mistake.

3. "Fixin' To" - When Tennesseans say they're "fixin' to" do something, it means they're about to do it soon. "I'm fixin' to grab some hot chicken for lunch."

4. "Tighten Up" - If someone tells you to "tighten up," it means they're advising you to get your act together or pay closer attention to something.

5. "Hot Chicken" - Speaking of hot chicken, this spicy fried chicken dish is a Tennessee specialty, particularly

famous in Nashville. Don't leave Tennessee without trying it!

6. "Vol" - Short for "Volunteer," it's a term often used to refer to the University of Tennessee's sports teams and their fans. If you're in Knoxville during football season, expect to hear this a lot.

7. "Smokies" - Locals refer to the Great Smoky Mountains as the "Smokies." It's a breathtaking national park on the border of Tennessee and North Carolina, known for its misty peaks and lush forests.

8. "Buggy" - In Tennessee, a "buggy" isn't a small vehicle; it's a shopping cart you push around in a grocery store.

9. "Holler" - This is a term for a small, often rural, valley in the Appalachian region. You might hear someone say they live up in the holler, meaning they live in a more remote area.

10. "Coke" - Like in many Southern states, "Coke" in Tennessee is a generic term for any carbonated soft drink. So, if you want a Pepsi or a Mountain Dew, just ask for a "Coke."

Now that you're equipped with some local language, you're ready to appreciate everything Tennessee has to offer. From the thriving music scene to the delectable cuisine, you'll interact with the people and learn about Tennessee's distinct personality.

Vaccinations

All visitors to Tennessee and the United States are advised to be vaccinated against hepatitis A and B. This is the most common infectious illness in the United States, and it may occur in any restaurant with poor cleanliness. Aside from minor annoyances such as unpleasant poison ivy and poison oak plants in the forests, the state has no severe health risks.

Tennessee is generally regarded as a safe place to visit. Visitors should be cautious when exiting late-night bars in Memphis and Nashville. Beale Street and Broadway may get quite boisterous at times, resulting in fights. Theft is a common problem in busy tourist areas, so don't leave anything expensive in your rental car. However, violent crimes and muggings are uncommon in Tennessee, so use caution.

Online accessibility

Tennessee has excellent internet connectivity. 99.9% of state inhabitants have access to wired or wireless internet at speeds of up to 10 Mbps. Despite the fact that these fast speeds allow users to perform almost anything online, 36.9% of Tennessee residents do not have access to the internet.

DSL is available to 90.4% of Tennessee residents. Cable internet is available in 86.8% of houses. Wireless internet is available to 99.3% of people. 24.8% of the population has access to fiber internet.

In addition, 47.7% of the population has three or more internet service providers.

There is no reason for Tennessee citizens to be without basic internet access.

Transportation

While all major cities in Tennessee have strong air connections, cross-state transportation is confined to Greyhound buses and private automobiles. The vast majority of visitors who intend to do any sightseeing in this city rent a car for the length of their visit. Interstate 40 extends from east to west through Tennessee, offering quick access to all major communities.

All major airports and the majority of large cities have rental vehicle companies with offices. The drive here is breathtaking, especially along Interstate 40, which passes through the scenic Tennessee River Valley.

Taxis are available in all of the state's main cities. Cabs are tough to hail on the street, so keep a few phone numbers at the ready and call for a ride. Checker Cab (+1-615-256-7000) is more well-known in Nashville than Metro Cab (+1-901-322-2222). Tennessee taxis use meters to calculate fares, which are frequently low for local journeys.

Trains and buses in Tennessee

Memphis is the only city in Tennessee served by Amtrak trains. It is located on the popular City of New Orleans line, which connects Chicago and New Orleans. The train is an excellent method to go to Memphis from either direction since the seats are comfortable and the view is breathtaking. Although the train is less expensive than a short regional flight, it is only suggested for those with plenty of time.

The cheapest and most convenient way to travel between Tennessee locations is via Greyhound bus or MegaBus. Greyhound is the most convenient means to go to the state from afar, whereas MegaBus only provides regional service. Both are affordable and comfy.

Holidays And Festivals

It's no surprise that music takes center stage at the majority of Tennessee's yearly festivals. This state is home to the most music festivals, including major highlights like Bonnaroo and Riverbend. There appeared to be something fun to do every weekend during this relaxed period between spring and fall. Tennessee's festivals are a great chance to immerse yourself in local culture and give your trip a unique flavor.

1. Tin Pan Alley's southern neighbor

Every March, this five-day Tennessee feast of songwriting and singing takes place in the music-loving city of Nashville. Hundreds of musicians, both well-known and emerging, travel to town to play and share their passion for music throughout the festival, which spans every venue and genre.

The River City Brewer's Festival Memphis opens the taps and serves craft beer in Handy Park every March for a full weekend of beer enjoyment. Every year, more than 75 brewers from throughout the country congregate in downtown Memphis for this well-known event, which kicks off the spring season. Because the park is so close to Beale Street, the party always overflows into the bars for live music and after-hours drinking.

2. Musical Festival on Beale Street

This excellent music festival kicks off the month of May in Memphis, which is a popular destination. It takes place in late April for three days and features some of the top bands on the scene performing on four distinct stages in Tom Lee Park. The ideal way to welcome spring is to sit on the Mississippi River's banks and listen to wonderful musicians.

Music and Arts Festival Bonnaroo
This biennial music event, which evokes long-forgotten Woodstock memories, is hosted on a 700-acre farm in

Manchester and attracts hundreds of thousands of fans as well as an all-star roster of Tennessee performers. The music ranges from techno to alternative rock and is accompanied by a beer festival, a comedy club, a theater, and other amusing creative elements. This is one of the most major music events in the country, held every June.

3. The Riverfront Music Festival

Every June, 500,000 people go to Chattanooga's riverfront park for nine days of incredible live music as part of the city's biggest festival. The program goes from dawn to sunset and requires six stages to accommodate approximately 100 artists. This is one of Tennessee's most prominent music events each year.

4. State Fair of Tennessee

For many people, the Tennessee State Fair is the highlight of the year. Every September, the State Fairgrounds outside of Nashville offer a 10-day jamboree of music, carnival rides, junk food, and limitless family fun. Spend the day networking and having fun with the family at Tennessee's gorgeous state fair.

Contact Numbers

- Crime in Progress: 911
- Crime or Suspicious Activity: 931-526-2125
- Crime Stoppers: 931-520-7867
- Downed Electrical Line: 931-526-7411 or 931-526-2125
- Fire Emergency: 911
- Gas Leak: 931-520-4427 or 931-526-9591
- Medical Emergency: 911
- National Poison Control Center: 800-222-1222
- Routine Police Call: 931-526-2125
- Water/Sewer Leak: 931-520-5227 or 931-528-5533
- *Road/Weather/Traffic Conditions :***511**

Budgeting Tips

Where to Stay on a Budget in Tennessee

One piece of advice I have for saving money on hotels is to travel during the off-season or shoulder season. When all of the tourists go, hotel prices fall substantially.

Hotels on a Budget

However, if you visit during the high season, you may be able to get cheap housing. Even in Tennessee's most popular tourist locations, you should be able to find reasonably priced lodgings for less than $65 per night. Whatever time of year you visit, Knoxville, Nashville, and Gatlinburg all have affordable accommodations.

Air B&B

If you want to save even more money, consider staying in an Air BnB rental. Rooms or entire homes/apartments should be available to rent for less than $45 per night.

Camping

If you're looking for the cheapest option for a hotel in Tennessee, consider camping. The state is OVERFLOWING with natural beauty. Indeed, my finest camping trip was a solo vacation to Tennessee many years ago.

You have the option of camping near your car and having access to facilities and showers, or you may choose a "backcountry" or "primitive" campground where you may have to travel to your campsite and may not always have access to drinking water or a toilet.
In general, if you wish to stay at an established campsite, you should budget between $15 and $35 per night. While reserving a campsite, you may be forced to pay a reservation fee, so keep that in mind as you plan your vacation.

Backcountry camping is not for everyone. It is, however, the least-priced option. Backcountry camping is typically completely free if you have the opportunity. If you don't want to go rustic camping every night of your trip to Tennessee, consider camping only once or twice. If you plan on spending a few days in a state or national park, now is an excellent opportunity to save money by backcountry camping.

Finding Cheap Food in Tennessee

Eating out in popular tourist regions is expensive. Overall, Tennessee is a moderately affordable destination, with many meals costing less than $10 per person. It is always possible to buy groceries and make your meals, which will greatly minimize your vacation expenses.

If you're looking for restaurants that provide excellent and economical meals, I've read a few great pieces on restaurants that serve tasty and inexpensive meals. All four articles are worthwhile reads that can help you save money when visiting Tennessee.

Free Attractions in Tennessee

Visit some of Tennessee's free attractions and activities to save money!

1. **Clingman's Dome**

Clingman's Dome, a popular tourist destination barely a half-mile from Gatlinburg, offers stunning views. The trail is short and paved, making this a straightforward journey.

2. **Hiking**

Wow, wow, and wow. The hiking in Tennessee is fantastic, and there are several route options. There are several types of trails, such as short trails, long trails, multi-day routes, and paved trails. Hiking is quite popular in Tennessee, especially in the east. I've produced a list of some of the most popular trails in the state. These are critical on the Chimney Tops Trail.

A 3.6-mile hike with substantial elevation change, but the reward is an amazing view.

3. **The Start of the Falls Trail**

Fall Creek Falls State Park is a popular 0.8-mile trail with moderate elevation change. This is a fantastic photographic spot.

4. **The Gorge Overlook Trail**

This gives a great view of the gorge and the cascade that flows into it. This is a 2.9-mile trail that is quite easy to navigate, making it appropriate for children and hikers of all levels.

5. **A view of Mt. LeConte from Alum Cave Bluffs.**

For YEARS, this has been on my list of things to do in Tennessee. The name of this route has been on my mind for a long time. A challenging 5.5-mile hike in the Smokies will reward you with breathtaking landscapes and panoramas. (Look up photos of these trails; they're stunning!)

6. <u>Charlie's Get-Together</u>

This is a tough hike with stretches along a stunning large rock path. When you get to the viewpoint, you may sit on a projecting chunk of the mountain and snap some stunning shots of yourself with the mountains in the background.

7. <u>Go for a drive in the Great Smoky Mountains National Park.</u>

The drive through the Smoky Mountains, especially in the fall, is spectacular. There are several locations to pull over and enjoy the view, you may stop for a picnic lunch at one of the picnic areas, and you can also take advantage of the short easy accessible hikes offered from some of the mountain pull-off points.

8. <u>Meet The Dolly's Stampede Horses</u>

Dolly's Stampede offers a horse stroll one hour before the events for FREE horse-watching.

9. **Take a stroll through the village.**

Walking around this medieval-looking neighborhood in Tennessee is a lot of fun. While you're there, you may go window shopping or grab a cheap bite to eat.

10. **Visit Douglas Lake**

Swim, relax, or bring a picnic lunch at Douglas Lake in the Great Smoky Mountains. (Alternatively, do all three!)

11. **Go on a Self-Guided Walking Tour.**

Take a tour around Chattanooga or Sevierville and check for all of your favorite sites if you're visiting.

12. **The Memphis Brooks Museum of Art.**

This Memphis museum is a "pay what you can" establishment. Enjoy great paintings without having to pay full price.

13. __Mud Island River Walk__

This is fantastic for kids! This park features a little shallow "river" built into the pathway into which children may dip their feet and play to their hearts' content. In my opinion, this is a terrific park concept.

The Knoxville Botanical Gardens is ranked tenth.

Enjoy the walking paths, historical structures, and, of course, the 40 or so acres of lush flora and animals.

14. __Ijam's Nature Center.__

I strongly advise you to pay a visit to Ijam's.

Printed in Great Britain
by Amazon

39776899R00076